HIM

Other books by

Pierre Alex Jeanty

Best-Sellers

HER.

HER Vol. 2

Unspoken Feelings of a Gentleman

To the Women I Once Loved

Other Books

Unspoken Feelings of a Gentleman II

In Love with You

Apologies That Never Came

Coming soon

HEart

HIM

Pierre Alex Jeanty

jeanius
PUBLISHING

Cover Design: Celia James
Editor: Sarah Plamondon & Carla DuPont

ISBN-13: 9781949191073

Jeanius Publishing LLC
430 Lee Blvd
Lehigh Acres, FL 33936

For more information, please visit:
Jeaniuspublishing.com
Pierrealexjeanty.com

<u>Schools & Businesses</u>

Jeanius Publishing books are available at quantity discounts
with bulk purchases.
For more information please email
contact@jeaniuspublishing.com

When I wrote HER, I wanted to empower women, wanted them to know that there are men out there who recognize, appreciate, and celebrate their strength. There are men who want to understand them.

After the book became a success and I published the second version, I felt like a little bit of my voice was drifting away from my original focus. I felt myself being put into the box that reads, **"Modern poets who only know how to glorify women."**

In the beginning, I started writing to be a voice that spoke for the broken men, the loving men, the growing men, and the good men. I wanted to speak for the men who are classified under 'all men are dogs,' when they themselves never or no longer believe in promiscuity and self-destructive lifestyles.

I started out writing to express my mistakes, my regrets, where I fell short with love and women, and how I grew from those things.

I am passionate about that; I am passionate about helping men who see themselves in my story to grow. Along the journey, I decided I wanted to reach women as well. Loving my wife pulled that out of me.

Don't get me wrong, I love uplifting women, and to know so many women HER has touched is beautiful.

Women ought to know that they are worthy of love, consistency, loyalty, respect, and so forth. They must also know that we aren't all bad, they aren't all good, always right, or always the victim.

I want men to get some glory and be understood as well.

I am a balanced human being who tries to do everything with balance.

HIM *is not as far different from*
HER *as the mirror of society*
paints it for their eyes to see...

I do not claim to know
the hearts of all men,
I only vow to express my inner
thoughts.

I will never

fight for the men

who can't be men

to women.

He feels,

He cares,

He breaks,

He knows pain,

He makes mistakes,

He grows,

He learns,

He heals,

He loves.

Maybe there is not a lack of
good men for women or good
women for men, but a lack of
people falling for those who are
meant to catch their hearts.
Somewhat like the good in this
world, the lack of it is easily
discovered by the eye; yet,
where it lies in abundance isn't
given enough credit.

Do you care about what's on his mind, or are you digging out of him reasons you should be on it?

Do you care about his happiness, or do you only care to search for your happiness inside of him?

Do you even care about his life, or are you making sure that you become his world and begging him to live as if you're the only thing in his universe?

How can you want to always be on his mind, want him to make you happy and only care for a life with you, when you barely care enough about his existence without you?

He was not made to become the living
definition of *a 'real man'* that you've
extracted from memes, tasted from
bitter tongues, and plastered on the
walls of your mind
because it fits into everything your ex
never was.
He is not trying to become '*real*' in the
eyes of a generation who cannot
separate truth from emotions,
and experience from reality.

He was created to be authentic to
genuine hearts, caring to loving souls,
and bear greatness into this world.

His being was knitted with integrity
and confidence, grown of good
character and valor.
His idea of 'a real man' is to fulfill the
image of what a good man ought to be
modeled after.

"A real man"

If his kisses taste everything like
honesty,
it does no good to speak
dishonestly of him simply because
all you've known of men
is the dishonesty they've poured
into your ears.

A man cannot be unworthy of trust
simply because men who looked like
him walked into your life and
slowly devoured yours.

He is weak for you,
but that does not mean he is weak.

He is strong for himself
but that does not mean it is his burden
to forever be the strength for both of
you.

*Love isn't always the easiest thing
to harvest.*
If this truth has settled in your
veins already, you must not act
blind to the contradictions that are
swirling in your breath
when you've grown angry at him
for not falling in love with you on
your timing.

You can't just shake a growing
tree saying, "*I am a good woman so
love me,*"
and expect fruits of love to just
fall.
How many seasons did your love
have to endure before it bore a
harvest?

I am always able to love,
I am simply unable to
always be loving.

There is a silent war in his mirror,
one with a history
that is out to conquer his mind.

There is a loud battle in his mind,
An, "Am I enough?" fight over his
manhood.

Am I tall enough?
Am I good-looking enough?
Am I successful enough?
Am I man enough?

Countless allies of his insecurities
bomb his happiness, attempting to
overpower everything good in him.
He is fighting an invisible crusade
that only the soul knows,
the spirit recognizes,
and the naked eye will easily miss.

"War Zone"

I am slowly merging into the lane
that was created for me,
slowly detaching myself from my
past
and peeling off these callouses
over my heart.

Men, too, are caterpillars
becoming butterflies.
They grow wings
and later become lions
who refuse to be misled by pride
and hunted by their ego.

If I cannot be cherished by you,

I will not become a burden,

I will become a lost treasure.

If I cannot be a blessing to you,

I will not become a curse.

I will become absent.

Many men who seem to have it
together are slowly breaking down,
constantly adjusting their grip as
they try to hold on.
They live clueless of how to
undress their ego
and be welcoming to helping hands
that are dying to grab them and
help them pull themselves up.
These men have learned to walk
this earth alone,
a beautiful thing that carries ugly
outcomes when a dead end is
reached.

"We all need bridges."

Him

I hope one day we mourn the
innocence stolen from the minds of
boys before they knew how to write
their name properly.

I do not say this to throw pity parties,
I say this to address the elephant in the
room that is slowly leaving no room for
men to breathe.

I am talking about the double
standards that treat my brothers as
nothing, while everything they do
becomes something that needs to be
talked about and protested.

I want to apologize to the men
who the boy in me once mocked for
being too loving,
for holding onto their virginity,
for having pure hearts,
for valuing commitment,
for befriending vulnerability,
for being loyal to one woman.

Only tongues of fools discover
reasons to mock the softness of
men and love in their voices.

Him

Don't mistake him for the boys
who try to find their way between
your legs; boys whose hearts only
see you as a piece of meat from
their menu of lust,
the perfect side piece.

He, however, is a man who is
hunting for something different,
a man searching for the love in
your soul,
the softness in your smile,
the courage in your voice,
the freedom in your laugh,
the calm of your touch.

Pierre Alex Jeanty

There are men who know when to
take it slow,
and men who know how to fake
their fall while their ten toes are
planted enough for them
to run away at any given time.

There are also men who cannot
keep themselves from indulging
when they find something good,
and some who know how to be
first obsessed,
then consistent with their
obsession.

Pace doesn't reveal the heart,
only character.

He is the type of man who does not
allow words of life to stall in the
back of his throat until they grow
dry of meaning.

Men like him can see the lack of
kind and loving words that travel in
and out of mouths daily.
Therefore,
he is overly expressive,
consistent at compliments,
overflowing with affection on
purpose.

He is only trying to create a little
balance in this world by being the
type of man many women don't get
a taste of.

"Can't you see that?"

Pierre Alex Jeanty

Women who pick men by their
appearance always set themselves
up for failure.
It is an injustice to let a man's
body keep you away from his *gold
mind*, and a heart where love is
buried.

Women who've decided whether or
not a man is worthy of their hearts
by how much room his pockets
have left,
digging with the hope that there's
enough gold inside
to arouse their hearts
have only robbed themselves of a
better life,
not the other way around.

Him

Let's be honest.
You didn't love him,
he was an escape out of your
loneliness,
your therapy for attention.
Yet here you are,
still trying to convince him that
your heart is shackled to his love,
that your love existed for his
existence.

And now he is running away,
you keep throwing more empty
words to keep him from being
willing to search for someone who
doesn't have to pretend.

"Liar"

To the boys who've had their
hearts ripped out of them and their
pride stomped on,
you tell them,
"Hurry up and heal so when you
date, you don't hurt our women."
You make sure they know that men
carrying pain are storms,
tornadoes, tsunamis, and volcanoes.

Yet to the girls you say, *"Queen, if*
he can't love you without flaw and
practice patience, let him go."

"Villains"

There's no fear in love,
they say.
I know it's true, but I must take my
time to make this truth bone of my
bones.
How do I swallow this truth when
my ears are full of, '*I love you's*'
from people who have given my
heart every reason to fear the next
lover?

There's no fear in love, they say,
but the only love I've ever seen
gave me these fears.

So bear with me, I am learning to
live through these terrible
experiences, slowly digesting them,
making myself ready to flush them
out.
I am determined make room for my
stomach to take in more truth as *my
truth.*

A man having no guidance is never
an excuse as to why he continues to
live a misguided life,
misleading women along the way.

But if we are being honest,
don't we live in a cause and effect
world?
Or do you only see a cause when
someone else is affecting you?

There is no sin in being logical and
no crime in not being an activist for
emotions.
There may be the lost opportunity
to be an empath when life summons
us for the job,
but we must never forget that
emotions,
more often than not,
are guilty of pushing us to the
wrong places which we never
should've ventured.

"Be their master."

You silence his concerns by raising
your voice
to voice yours,
yet complain about how his silent
treatment is causing injury.

Can't you see that it's the remedy
to your neglect?
Two wrongs don't make a right,
but a wrong cannot call another
wrong
right.

Him

Brother,

the weight of your existence cannot

fit into your pocket.

Your wallet shouldn't define your

life just because there are women

who do not mind living in it.

Empty

I do not know how to be in love with you.

I do not know how to be in love.

I've been told to hide my feelings in my bones,

so only when I become a skeleton will they be close

to being seen.

See, even death won't be enough light to find them,

not until every part of me is broken and ground

down, until the marrow is exposed along with

everything I've ever felt, every part of my existence

crushed to nothing.

I am not dead inside, I am simply empty.

Those who visited my heart before you

told me that this was not normal.

They consistently reminded me that they could not

find reason to live in a home without colors,

without furniture,

doors that were never opened,

and a yard with dying grass that seemed to keep

snakes away and everyone else along with them.

This temple only knows me,

it only knows abandonment, a

nd it knows nothing special besides pain.

Words of love slip through my teeth,

yet you don't hear it from my heart.

It is not pretense,

people with empty hearts speak wishes quite often.

I do not lie about love,

I am merely still practicing how to say it in a way

that helps my heart join the chant.

I am not happy with this temple.

I am still cutting down the trees planted by the

demons God drove out when I begged Him to park

Himself inside my heart,

making way for the sun to find me.

I am not a hypocrite,

I just don't know how to love.

Never did I hurt her and not feel
twice the pain,
as if every low blow to her was an
uppercut to my rib.

Quite the contrary,
men who are truly on the road of
love cannot hit and run.
They either run,
then get hit,
or hit,
then walk
with heavy legs,
aching hearts,
and regret chasing after them.

"It's never easy."

When loving a man like him
becomes something you cannot
bring yourself to cherish,
you must let him go.

Let him go without tying an
invisible string of hope to his leg,
slowly reeling him back in
while you figure out if you are
ready to be loved by a man like him
or not.
Let his heart find freedom to learn
the name of a woman who will
cherish it without hesitation.

Unearth his roots before you pass
judgement on the fruits he bears.
Instead,
dig to find what kind of soil he was
planted in,
the way he was watered,
who became the sunlight to his eyes
etc.,
to learn what type of tree he is and
understand why he grows the
harvest you see.
You must care enough to reach
deep.

We don't know anything about
anyone with whom we only walk on
shallow ground.

Him

I am nothing like the pretentious
lovers who came before I found my
way to you.
Our voices do not sound the same,
our intentions don't come from the
same place,
our burdens do not weigh the same.

I say this to remind you not to trap
this new love of ours in the box
that your old loves handcrafted.
I do not look like them,
so, don't look for me in the mirror
of your pain.

He does not let water run freely

from his eyes

because he is afraid that they will

create rivers that will soon form

lakes,

then oceans of pity for him to

drown in.

That is why his cry for help is dry.

Do you know what it feels like not
to know how to do the only thing
you must know to do?

Have you tasted the frustration,
smelled the fear,
or felt the disappointment that cut
off your limbs while you tried to
make your way somewhere?

This is his battle with love;
to want to love,
yet know nothing about it; to be
thirsty for affection, yet not know
how to drink from the cup by whom
it's served; to be hungry for
consistency, yet not know how to
enjoy the taste of it.

None of us are without a past.
It's unfortunate that he had been a
dog during the days he was the pet
to his lust,
but that man has grown beyond his
foolishness.

To hunt down and kill the lion
that is climbing out of him
with reminders of what he once
was, *is cruel.*

As a man graduates from living like
a king to being a king,
please do not unbury his less
honorable days to gain ground on
him.

Are you kidding me?
There are guys out there who will
not find it childish to love another
man's child.

As a matter of fact,
there are some looking to be more
of a father to the fatherless.

"Conversation with a single mom."

Brothers,

we too are emotional creatures.

We let anger carry the tone of our

emotions.

We let silence take all of our words,

stealing our voices and desire to

ask for what our souls need.

We let rejection steal every bit of

adventure and risk in us.

Whether or not we admit it,

we are tortoises;

tough on the outside,

soft on the inside, and only move at

our pace.

There is no righteousness in rage;
it only creates fires to burn things
down.
Do not let that rage be your fuel,
it'll only give you a drive for the
wrong things or help you spark
things the wrong way.

I am not a rebound,

I am the man who refuses to stay

on the sideline when the ball is in

my court.

I actually want to be a teammate

and win with her at this thing called

love.

"I am your last quarter."

Good men have always existed and
will always occupy space on this
earth.
There will be those who will blind
themselves of reasons to give them
credit,
but the good they bring to this
world will always better the soil of
this planet;
they will always outweigh the bad.

When I limit a woman to '*just friends,*'
they call it being mean.
They call me a puppet of immaturity because
I am letting a good one walk.
They say I am guilty of misleading her,
and call it being afraid of commitment and
addicted to chasing less.
They crucify me for not being a fan of their
pick.

Yet,
when I am the prisoner of the friend-zone
and proclaim that I am being overlooked,
they tell me to grow up and accept the fact
that she doesn't want me.

She says, "*I don't want a relationship,*" yet
texts me the sweetest words,
luring me to invest quality time and
occasionally brush her lips against mine.

I am supposed to see those things as
nothing, recognize those actions filled with

interest and those misleading behavior as friendship events.

How easy it is to believe that a man in the friend-zone is on his way to becoming a predator, while the man who guards the friend-zone is meant to be her prey?

He does not see you as his
conquest.
To him,
you are not land to colonize and
leave in poor condition
to forever be a slave to his touch,
under the occupation of his lies.
There are no oppressive tactics
hidden in his words.
He is here to honor your roots,
find beauty in your culture and
become loyal to the queen in you.

"There are kings in the deck."

"How did we fall out of love?"
she asked.
"The same way ashes are made," I
replied.
"We never fed our flames."

The beautiful words that swim out of his
crooked teeth are not the words of a
crook.
They do not come from a crooked heart;
they are perfect words floating their way
out of the mouth of the imperfect.
They are words of a sinner with a pure
heart and good intentions.

You are a woman's prayer,
the miracle she patiently waits for,
the priceless reward that she will
never give away.

Your love for her will be cherished,
you cheering her on will be more
than proof to her eyes that you are
here to build.

She will not betray you,
she will honor every bit of you,
she will not condemn you for things
you aren't blameworthy of.
To let the bad you've tasted take
this truth away from you,
is to be deceived.

Here you are, trying to convince me
that not trusting easily is the
devil's hold on what we have, yet
your words slowly became the very
image of why I am slow to trust.

"Lucifer, the angel."

Let me be the simp who commits,

the punk who is loyal,

the guy who is affectionate,

the softy who cries,

the stupid who is vulnerable,

the holier than thou who is

monogamous.

Let me be whatever your fear and

ignorance gives name to.

Call me whatever gives rest to your

misery,

It is not strong enough to stop me

from loving being in love and

becoming a loving man.

You are not any less special for
being a man.
Women are magical; but you too,
my friend, are a miracle this world
needs.
The existence of the moon is as
important as the existence of the
sun,
the soil has no more importance
than the flower,
your hand has no more importance
than your arm.
Men and women are blessings in
their own ways.

Light has always had the ability to drive
out darkness, I've been told.

It's easy for me to believe this when my
chocolate skin was always preferred
second compared to the boys whose skin
was like the sun, shining upon the faces of
the girls my age.
To them, I was the darkness creeping its
way into their presence, while the light-
skinned boys were the gold they were
looking for, the sunshine they needed.

I had to live in the shadows and pray that
I would get my shot, only to watch the
trigger be pulled on my heart because I
was not quite the preferred shade.
It was then I started learning that despite
the heaven I can offer, some fallen angels
dressed in yellow flesh would always be
their favorite paradise.

"Dark Boy"

How can he know how to love you
when you are clueless about how to
love yourself?
Giving a man a job that you cannot
do shouldn't make him
incompetent.
You've failed at it, why must you
toss away the credit he deserves for
trying?
Why don't you help him study you,
open your soul for him to learn
from the pieces of you that you do
know how to treat well?

Perhaps that could be a start to
both of you learning to let love
have its way with the two of you.

They say,

"She is more than an eye candy,
she is soul food."

I agree

And me...

"I am more than a snack,
I am a full course meal
made from a chivalrous recipe."

Pierre Alex Jeanty

There are men who will not forfeit
happiness for fleeting moments of
excitement.

Those are the men who have tasted the
type of love that satisfies them, yet
they could never become full on it.

Those are the men who find reasons to
call
their woman beautiful daily.

Those are men who prefer to be slaves
to love rather than live as masters of
lust.

Manhood was not stolen from you, only
parts of you have been explored and
exploited by enemies who have presented
themselves as friends.
Those parts of you are not meant to be
colonized by darkness, they are not meant to
remind you that you are weak and useless.
Dear boy,
you cannot walk on this earth with the
weight of such a past pinning you down.
Climb I tell you,
climb out of the cave of, " *Why me?*"
Crawl out of the jungle of, *"Do I deserve to
live?"*
Do not let their evil acts make you out to be
a lifeless soul.
There is strength on the other side; there are
rivers of joy, there is a field of smiles, there
are houses made out of love, and there is
freedom on the other side.
You must get to the other side.
You must not grow cold and numb, it will
only keep your legs from ever truly growing
forward.

And yes, they may consider you less of a
victim than the girls who've been chewed
apart by this sin, and that will always make
it harder to spit it out.
Let the truth find its way out of your mouth
and breathe; you can rise without being
acknowledged.
Rise my boy, rise.
Grab the hands of God and fly out of your
horrid past.

"Molestation"

Him

The mirror is not reflecting failure,
you are not worthless.
You stare into your own eyes,
speak words of life into yourself,
care for yourself.

Your mind, body, and soul are tired
of believing they are less than
great.
You are not a worthless seed on
this earth just because you haven't
seen what your life will reap.

When you find her,
give her the keys to your smile,
access to your heart,
allow her to hear the voice of your
deepest thoughts,
introduce her to your fears.

How can she offer you the love you
deserve when you only speak to her
through the cracked doors of your
heart without inviting her inside?

The best way for the pain to end is
to live through it.
There's heaven on the other side of
the hell that is in your way.
There's a lake of peace on the
other side of this drought.
There are canals of happiness all
over the land across the way.
Please get to the other side.
Please do not sacrifice your life to
this pain,
it will only give the pain a key to
burst through the doors and
terrorize those you love as well.
You are better than you believe
right now,
you are more loved than it seems,
and death doesn't deserve you
right now.
Make him earn it at the end.
I love you.

"Suicide, you evil thief."

He has heard that he is not good
enough so many times, that your
addition is only an echo.

You've given birth to this idea that
showing a man you can fight back
is power to win him over,
yet he never tried to put up a fight
in the first place.

So, you throw words at him to land
blows at his insecurities.
It doesn't work that way.
You can't love him in the same way
that those before him falsely loved
you.

In a world where far too many will
wish failure upon him and shove
their doubts down his throat until
he is full with enough of their
opinions
to vomit out his dreams,

be his cheerleader,
be his supporter,
be at least the one person who
holds their teeth tight so he isn't
bombarded by more unwanted
opinions.
If you cannot be the one who
believes in him,
at least be the one who does not
voice their lack of support.

Even if he was God,

you would still deem him to be

Lucifer because he was born in the

flesh of man.

It's not his fault that all you've

known of men is that they are the

best of sinners.

Him

Perhaps you are not his secret,
but his protected treasure.

Perhaps he isn't at fault;
instead it is your trust issues and
insecurities stirring up trouble,
clouding your mind with the belief
that social media validation is what
will prove that he isn't hiding you.

There are some who crave a private
life in an overexposed generation.
There are people who are silent
about their business so they don't
have to master the art of drowning
out unnecessary noise.

In the shadow of this hero
who seems tough as nails,
there is a boy who stares at those
in love
like the last cookie in the jar,
trying to wash out the strong taste
of weakness from his tongue.
This hero has played the coward
and failed far more times than the
lips can number.

Him

He is the epitome of what they say
doesn't exist:
A black man,
a single dad,
and a business owner
climbing out of the box of
prejudice.
He is destined for something big
despite what small minds believe
about him.

You may use your body to cast
spells and throw nets with your
appearance, but this fella here is
looking for more than bait to the
eyes.
Despite how many colorful fish
float on my explorer page and swim
past my eyes,
I will need more than that
temptation to click, because I want
more from the ocean.

"I want a mermaid."

I have learned that if you spend
enough time letting your eyes
indulge in the perfection of women
clothed with filters and make-up,
showcasing themselves on the
internet,
it is easy to become disconnected
from cellulite,
outgrow the idea of body hair,
and be unwilling to face a face with
acne.
The line between skin and
presentation will be blurred.

I am not condemning the women
who do such things but reminding
you that you can lose your grip on
what a woman truly looks like when
you are often looking at them in an
altered form.

*"The commercial always looks
different from the reality."*

Is he really the coward who you
claim he is?
How can he lack courage for being
unwilling to commit to a woman
who does not want to learn the
meaning of healing?

Why do you call him lame for not
wanting to force a woman to break
out of her prison of bitterness?

Why do you want him to weigh
himself down with unnecessary
responsibilities?

You tell him he is wrong for
running away, yet you tell women
who refuse to carry these types of
burdens to drop them and keep on
walking.

We, too, mourn our days of
singleness.
The craving for affection,
companionship, and love is
something we too desire.
We may not be willing to admit that
we want love, but all of us thirst
for it and are in of need it.

It is true that a queen without a
king is still a queen.
It is equally true that a king
without a queen is still a king.
But a king and a queen seated on
the throne is how you build a
beautiful and lasting kingdom on
love's continent.

"There's enough space for both."

His heart wasn't made to be a
remedy to the broken,
nor a hospital for the heartless.
These are demands they ask of him,
not what makes him a man.

It is not a woman's detective work,

her aging beauty,

her mesmerizing curves,

her talent beyond the curtains,

not even her carrying life for him

that keeps a man in love.

It is becoming the apple of his

heart,

the flower of his eyes,

his sunshine, and his star

that will do so.

Men in love don't need other

reasons to stay.

Him

As a man, I think I've earned the right to say
that we are deeply offended when we hear the
voices of women with politician-tongues and
wavering truth speak about us.

Some of them loudly claim that we are weeds
infecting God's green earth,
while in secret they mourn the missing touch of
a man.

Some join the chants,
reciting all the things men say and do wrong
while the insides of their ears itch for words of
comfort from a man.

Some create clever arguments as to why we are
all bad, debating how almost none of us are
different.
While some keep their fingers crossed and hope
a loving man will cross their path.

Please, understand that constantly pointing out
men's wrongs isn't an effective way to
convince them they must be better.

There are some of us who love doing better.
To live behind the curtain of hypocrisy is to
bury your chances of finding the man you
desire.

*"You're throwing stones at those of us who
want to help you win the war."*

He is still breaking off the chains of
foolish beliefs this world shackled
onto his mind,
unlearning the false idea of
manhood society has shoved down
his throat.
He is still studying the art of
becoming a man in a world of boys.
Be patient with him.

You throw short answers,
indirect hints,
and reverse psychology at him with
the hope that he will respond
exactly how you want.
Can't you see the confusion in
saying, *"It's okay,"* when it's not?
Hoping it will convince him that he
needs to dig deeper and realize that
it's not okay?
You cannot keep growing angry at
him for misinterpreting hints and
reading outside the lines instead of
in-between.
Although I do agree that he must
learn you enough to read between
the lines, I must also say that
communication itself is never a
remedy,
it is only healthy communication
that keeps love stories on the same
page.

Brother,

women are beautiful creatures.

It's hypocrisy to think so,

yet perform the ugliest acts against

them.

"Practice what you believe."

It wasn't until I realized that
beautiful was not a word to
describe the shape of a woman,
but a term used to define who she
is, what her hearts holds,
and who she aspires to be,
that I found reasons to fall in love.

If you ask me,

the women I know want their men

cooked with the right amount of

sensitivity, sprinkled with affection,

a few tablespoons of bad,

and seasoned enough to provide a

sense of security.

They become salty when there is

too much sensitivity,

suffocated by unhealthy amount of

affection, not enough good, and too

much fire in them.

The type of man I've seen they

prefer from the menu are slow

cooked meals that some women

think come cooked in microwaves as

hot pockets.

You become the poster child for a
'*What Good Men Do*' campaign that
is funded by broken women who
want their voices to be heard.
You don't listen to their voice,
but instead try to silence ours by
making all of us (men) guilty for
crimes some of us know nothing of.
You say men do this, men do that,
giving PowerPoint presentations
about what makes men terrible.
Here's a word for you, oh modern
knight:
You're a man just like us.
Aren't you good?

*"Good men who always talk about
how men are bad, aren't as good
as they think."*

If that man who has stolen your
attention and secured your interest
complements you,
compliment him.
Feed that man's confidence;
it will starve his ego faster
than your method of not looking
too thirsty.

I am not searching for '*just like a man*' characteristics in a woman.
There is something about women that only women can bring to the table; something special that they should embrace and nurture.
If I'm going to fall in love with a woman, I want her to own her womanhood,
stand bold in her own beauty, and thrive in her own strength without ever using a man's measuring stick.
Just being a woman is powerful enough.

They say if you stroke his ego, it'll
make it hard for him to stay.
He will come and go because
you've made him feel too important
and too loved.

I could not disagree more.
If you do not feed the dog that you
love, it will die.
If you do not water the plant that
you love, it will die.
If you do not give affirming words
to the man you love, his spirit will
die.

Your bad experience is
brainwashing you with the wrong
concepts of love.

"Fear is so dang loud!"

There's enough love in his heart to
love every single piece of you.
For the most part,
it will not show through romantic
gestures.
It will creep through his subtle
attempts,
it will scream through his work
ethics and hunger to give you the
world,
it will be loud in his consistency,
and
it will present itself as loyalty.
Many men are lovers who have no
clue about romanticism.

How can you be the woman of his
dreams when your heart cannot
gain enough strength
to be his back bone while he
navigates through his reality,
reaching for his dreams?
Showing him your support is a child
of the love that must come with
wanting to be in his life.
If you cannot become pregnant
with such motivation,
how can you be the woman of his
dreams?

There will always be men who want
everyone in their life to know
there's a woman in their world,
and there will always be other men
who want everyone in the world to
know they have a woman in their
life.

In better words, there are men in
love and there are men who want
everyone to know they are giving
love a shot.

In better words than the better
words before,
there are men who love for love,
and men who wouldn't appear as
great of lovers without the internet.

There is not a bone in him that
finds women being seeds of
pornography acceptable.
There's no appetite in him to see
the beauty of sex and women be so
perverted for the right price.

Sweetheart, beautiful, and honey
are bait sometimes thrown by males
who aren't looking to catch the
love in the hearts of women
searching for it.
Those men always claim they have
bigger fish to fry than to be in
relationships, and everything about
their attempt smells fishy.
However, there are many of us who
use them innocently.
There are many men who do not
have hidden agendas when they
speak these words.
We don't all hide traps underneath
our tongues and blend salt with our
sweet words.

"Double Meaning"

"What you don't do, another man will and steal her heart," they say.

What more can I do than to love her with my all?
Why should I try to protect something that wants to be taken away from me?

How is it my responsibility to make sure someone's legs are heavy enough not to walk out, especially when hard times visit us and their heart isn't loyal enough to make sure there are no unlocked doors for their favorite thief to come in?

I say, *"You will always lose what isn't meant to be yours."*

He loves too early but falls in love
too late.
What a contradiction, you must
think; but only to those whose
pasts have locked their lips and
their brains have convinced them
that anything too early is another
step into the dungeon of heartbreak
and another marriage with pain.

He patiently held a seat for love in
his heart.
He waited for the season when he
might harvest it,
yet became so paralyzed by fear
that he did not realize that he never
watered it.

Some of your sisters are using
every ounce of breath in their
voices to protest men like him,
yet you applaud his bad habits.
You call it an alpha male at work,
while you crucify me for being
too good, too loving, and a little
too unmaterialistic.

"Gold Diggers"

Closure came to his door steps
when he realized that you will never
judge his character by who he is
now, but rather who he was to you.
He finally met the understanding
that one will never find hope inside
someone who sees no hope in them.

Here you are, making accusations
that you cannot prove,
blaming him for things your friends
assume and your insecurities
declare.

The burden of trying to prove to
you that he is not the devil's first
born or filled with bad motives
is getting too heavy to carry.

You can't keep putting him down
and expect him to stand up for you.
How does one stand up for a
relationship when they are
constantly being pushed down?

"Tired"

Seeing you with someone new is
fire under his skin.
It never gets old.
He hides his true feelings, hoping
the flames that once lit up like the
sky on Fourth of July will quickly
die out.
His wishes can't seem to come true,
whether it be wanting what once
was to become what is,
or for what is to become what was
to him.
However, getting over you is
moving at the slowest pace
possible.
Therefore, on his face is a mask
made of pretense. He dresses up his
hurt in, "I don't give a dang about
that," and outfits himself with
bright smiles.

"I don't need her."

Him

Women make mistakes too.
Women hurt men too.
Women play men and manipulate
them too.
To some I am stating the obvious,
but to others I am shooting flares
of myths that will make their blood
boil because they've been wronged
more than they've been wrong.
The truth still stands.
Women make mistakes too.
Women hurt men too.
Women play men and manipulate
them too.

We do not give women's existence
meaning,
we can only be part of why they are
more meaningful.
It's no different than how they also
give our lives more meaning and
make the sacrifices make sense.

He is searching for a woman who
will help him find more peace than
he has ever known in any
relationship.

Peace that will help him unwind
when he gets home,
help him take off his
responsibilities,
unbutton the thoughts of that last
email or deadline,
loosen up those tired arms,
and untie the stress of dealing with
clients.

Life itself is a burden sometimes,
who wants their special someone to
make it harder?

I am not deaf to your needs,
I am tired of only hearing your
demands.
I have never known love to find
roots in fields of the selfish.

Far more than enough times,
women underestimate the power of
just listening to the words that
crawl out of a man's mouth.

In the same manner, they
themselves just want their words to
be heard sometimes without an
answer, suggestion, or solution
waiting to be spoken on the other
end.

"Venting"

Son,
there is nothing wrong with falling
for eye candy, but the model you're
desperately after will have to be
filter-less in your presence.
You will not be able to Photoshop
her true character, and she will
have to become the role model for
your child.

You must keep this in mind and not
let your eyes be the only things
leading you to love.

There are venomous words of the
ego, and words that leak out of the
jaws of fear.
There's a difference.

They do not have the same hunger.

The ego is desperate for bedroom
points while fear will drive
insecurities to lay good things
aside.
They can make a man seem both
cold and careless,
but
they are traits that exist in different
types of men for different
purposes.

He may have been the villain once,
but to accuse him of crimes he did
not commit is not to bring justice to
love, it's being a terrible judge.

Him

He will shed
a thousand tears
before you
see him cry.

I must admit,

there are times I complete sentences

in my head and only speak the first

words to you,

yet expect you to know where to

put the period.

There are times I am terrible at

explaining, yet expect to be

understood.

Forgive me for those times, I am

working on fixing the signal of my

communication.

I'm working on pressing send to

more texts, and actually grabbing

thoughts out of my head and typing

them in the reply box or saying

them for face-to-face.

"Incomplete thought."

He has been told to accept your size
regardless, treat your arrogance as
an attitude to endure,
and your fire like a light.
But you,
you've been told not to settle for
fat guys, or guys whose other
package doesn't meet your
requirements.
You've been taught not to consider
your size, but to consider the size
of his wallet.
You've been taught not to be
tolerant to his flaws yet expect for
him to find the beauty in yours.
"How is this fair?"

Yes,

he is looking for love.

Yes,

he wants to settle down without

settling.

Yes,

he is looking to build a family and

grow old with his life partner.

Yes,

he needs oxygen to live.

"If it's obvious, let it be true."

The strategy you come up with while you
hold meetings with your girls, trying to
find the best way to get what you want out
of me, will not help.
Games are for kids who do not know what
they are searching for.
What I want is for you to make up your
mind and tell me the truth.
Misleading hints mixed with indirect words
in hopes of drawing me into a land of
indecisiveness, isn't it?
I cannot keep trying to find truth in your
lies.
"If you do this, he'll do that.
If you do that, he'll do this," are ways to
trap a man who doesn't want to be caught.
How many of those girls you're listening
to have kept the man they used their hard-
to-get game on?
I am already caught,
I am only trying to catch your drift.

There are times when it is my ego
searching for its position in
leadership.
There are other times
when I just want logic to make our
decision rather than following the
counseling of our emotions.
Sometimes I am right,
sometimes I am wrong.
Even you hate admitting you're
wrong too.

"Human Nature"

You cannot keep putting words into
the mouth of his silence and grow
angry when you feel that you've
wasted too much time on him,
drunk on assumptions.

He may not yet be good at
communicating, but he is great at
answering questions.
When he says he is fine,
keep yourself from treating it as if
it's your version of "I'm fine."
"Believe him."

Out of your mouth came, "If we
ever separate, show me that you
love me by fighting for me."
But when I fought, you stormed out
of the ring and took one of the
judge's seats,
waiving your card with a list of all
the wrong moves I made.
You beat all the hope out of me,
pulled back and shoved me away,
only to hint that if I did not get up
and endure, that I was not meant to
be.
I am willing to go through hell to
reach heaven, but I am not willing
to run to the hell that I want to be
heaven.

He was the one who got away...

before she realized that time waits
for no woman either.

We are meant to protect and serve,
brothers. If we abuse our authority,
how do we expect trust and love to
be always mentioned alongside our
names?

All that might of yours was not
given to you to overpower our
women, but to overpower anything
that is meant to destroy you and
them.

Him

The games, the hobbies,

the time spent with his friends,

is escapism.

When you become what he escapes

from more than you are a part of

his escapism,

that is when there is trouble in the

pot.

Pierre Alex Jeanty

His idea of love is to do whatever is
necessary for you to have whatever
is necessary.

"Labor of love."

Him

I will honor your every need,
but I will not sacrifice for all your
wants.
Not all wants need to be attended
to.

His legs don't know how to run

from commitment anymore,

they only know how to chase love.

There are women who are trying to
do more squats,
get better skin tone,
longer hair,
and take more trips
EVERY – FREAKING – WHERE.
Acquire a taste for a woman who is
more than breasts and thighs,
who is more concerned about the
size of her heart than the size of
her butt.
Get yourself one whose idea of true
beauty isn't measured on the ruler
of society's approval chart,
a woman who doesn't find
traveling from bed to bed fulfilling.
There are plenty of beautiful people
in this day and age,
but a beautiful heart ought to be
the priority.

We are tired of our silence

being misinterpreted

as well...

Him

There will always be fools who let
go of good women
and spend the rest of their days
asking for forgiveness.
Alike, there will always be men who
know the difference between a good
woman, and the perfect woman for
them.
Those men spend a lot of time
watering the good woman who is
perfect for them.

Blue balls should never make way
for purple marks and bruises on the
temple of our women.
The pain of restrained excitement
cut short does not grant us access
to what we long for.
We must learn not to put our hands
on what does not belong to us,
simply because we think it is
inviting,
simply because we think we should.

"Rape can't be justified."

He is the exact reason why you
shouldn't judge a book by its
cover.
The title he shows is false,
his pages are written in Braille,
the stories are allegorical, and
'The End' sometimes means there
are more pages in another volume.

A good woman may not find it
burdensome to honor the survivor
in him,
but the right woman will make way
for her voice to reach the
conqueror in him.

Him

There will be times I hide these
feelings to hide the hurt from you.

There are men, and there are
wolves tucked in men's clothing.
He is not a wolf for wanting to
clean up the blood that is dripping
from your heart.
How can he be,
if he isn't acting like a vampire,
feasting on every drop and sucking
every ounce of life out of you?
Instead, he is bandaging it up with
his words, his kisses, his love.
Call it what it is.

When you read about women
overcoming the indoctrination of
major corporations and society
against their natural beauty,
understand that he is also
overcoming a false narrative of
manhood that's been spoon fed to
him.
It's a narrative that causes many of
you to say, *"All men do is destroy
hearts and walk away."*
There are standards that he is
demanded to meet as a man that are
only rinsing his mind of his own
identity.

"War knows no side."

Death does not take exceptional
men completely.
It may take their soul from this
earth, but not their legacy.
When you have impact, it goes
beyond mortal boundaries.

Brother,

to trust the image of manhood

created by a society that has

villainized this gender, is to drink

poison while expecting it to be

medicine to your soul.

When a man understands how rich
he is when he has time,
he will prefer spoiling his loved
ones with moments, over his care
for a hefty inheritance.
It is the misunderstanding that we
will have time later that causes us
to lay aside beautiful things now
carrying the mindset that we will
behold their beauty once we do not
have to worry about the bills.
Time invested into things that
money can't buy will always reap a
bigger return than anything else.

I am a good man despite what you
believe about putting the words
'good' and 'man' together.

I am a good man despite how much
the self-proclaimed good men use
our failures to profit off of women.

I am a good man despite how
influential the bad men are.

Good men are not those who carry
that title for a trophy of
acceptance, they are those with
good hearts and loving souls who
are chasing the righteous life.

I may not have always been a good
man, but my past and I aren't
friends.

When I shouted "Yes!" to you,
did you know it had thousands of
'No's' that had been whispered to
other women?

I cannot see how the tongues of my
brothers can find the strength to
call women by names that only
degrade them.
It's as if there aren't enough
words in the human language to
say "beautiful" instead of "B...,"
enough words to say, "Honey"
instead of "H...,"
enough words to say; "Sweetheart"
instead of "S...."
The list goes on.
The dictionary has far more than
enough words that can be great
substitutes for common words with
tasteless meanings.

I cannot understand how my sisters
found ways to justify these terrible
titles men call them, only to make
those words into nicknames that
their mouths know between friends.
Only if they knew that what they
accept will set the tone for what
many others will speak to them.

He feels deeply as a man.
Perhaps it is the reason why it
takes so long for him to express
things.
The thoughts and feelings are
making their way from a far-off
place, before they ever find their
way out through his lips.
There are lands and seas to cross
before his heart gets on board to
be united with love.

Why are you allowed to act
defensive and be emotional, but
when it comes to me, you call it
'being a puppet to my fragile male
ego?'

"Sensitive"

I am too strong to let anything
someone says pull emotions out of
me that should remain buried.
Somehow, for the one who makes
me weak,
I lose power.
Their words can cut into parts I
never knew existed.
Their actions can awaken the worst
in me.

And the pain that I've known faded
with every moment spent with you,
with every "I love you" my ears
captured from your lips,
with every drop of affection, you
poured into my cup.

"Undressing my heart."

Him

He is rare.

The more you treat him as ordinary,

the more you become blind to that.

Maybe he is still warming up to love
and trying to put out the flames of
betrayal that were left burning
inside of him.
Fires rarely end with the first blow,
they only die after many.

When her face isn't decorated,
when she isn't dressed her best,
when her favorite perfume isn't on,
and no smile is upon her face,
that is the best time to find out
whether your interest is true, or
lust is recruiting again.
Everyone is lovable and easy to
chase when they are wearing the
best version of themselves.

And when the demons he once knew
came to drag him back to his past,
he fought,
grabbing onto every fruit of peace
that had traveled through his
Adam's apple unto God, reminding
himself that he had survived hell
and there was no going back.
He fought to remain better;
to unbury the best version of
himself every day.

When you catch false promises
exiting out of your mouth, ask them
to turn back.
If you cannot and your effort isn't
willing to join the ride,
you must learn to keep your words
from being formed.
People deserve the truth out of
your lips.
Anything else is disrespectful.

The longer you live as if you don't
need him as a man, the more you
make him believe that exact truth.
No one finds enough comfort to
stay where they don't feel needed.

Treating people like you don't need
them only rushes them to find
someone who does.

Brother,

there is admiring a beautiful
creature, then there is assaulting
her with your eyes.
In looking and not touching, the
imagination still allows you to
touch every single part of a woman.
There is no harm in that, you say,
but shouldn't *your* woman be the
center of your imagination?
And you without a woman, you say
the same, but many thoughts
become words and actions.
Therefore, make sure that your
thoughts remain harmless.

The things your insecurities bark at
you are not things my eyes even
notice.
I don't care about your eye lashes,
the shape of your eyebrows,
the size of your nose,
the way your toes are aligned,
the tone of your skin,
or the natural, yet hidden
imperfections of your body.
I pay more attention to the things
you pay less attention to:
your selflessness,
the drive you have to impact the
world, how caring you are towards
certain things and people.
Stretch marks never scarred my
mind, and I can't even remember
what cellulite is.
Please let go of the weight of
insecurities that aren't even worth
naming.

I will show you how much a man
can love you in many different
ways, so that when another man
tries to use "I love you" as a trap
to capture your ears, you will be
able to differentiate the voice of
love from the tone of manipulation.

"Being a loving father."

If only he took the time to tell you
about every single opportunity that
came his way to betray the relationship.
But he does not find pleasure in telling
you how many women tried to cross
the boundaries.
When he was a lost boy, he used to
love the attention of the women who
did not respect relationships. It dug up
examples for his woman to see that
other options were knocking.
It was a fear tactic, a way of having
the upper hand, he once believed.

But now,
they aren't worth mentioning, they
aren't worth entertaining, his attention
is committed to this relationship and
staying grounded in love.
"This is what maturity does to people."

So, you expect him to turn a blind
eye to your obvious maltreatment.
"He is a man. Therefore he should
suck it up and take it like a man,"
you say to justify your actions.
Love may be blind,
but it is not that blind.

*"Call it what you want, but you
won't see love in wrongdoings."*

He is over you,

not because he found someone,

but because he found himself.

<u>Common plot known as uncommon:</u>

I saw a girl flirting with a group of men
say, *"He isn't all that. He can't handle me.
The only reason I'm with him is because
he gives me what I want,"* as a response to
one of them saying, *"He can't treat you
like I can."*

She then continued her narrative saying,
*"He is lame. I've got better guys after me.
He is too nice."* As she relayed this to her
girls, none of them found reason to
interrupt and ask, *"Then why are you with
him?"*

Later on in his presence, in the middle of
an argument with no foundation, she said,
*"How can you say you love me, but you
can't even get this or that for me? You're
not even a real man; not man enough for a
woman like me."*

He left her place, clueless as to what he
needed to do for his woman to see that
pleasing her heart was enough. The weight

of confusion slowly lured his thoughts into debating whether or not he was enough, causing anger to rise in him and war to rise in his mind.

Meanwhile, she called in that alpha male who showed up to be the perfect display of how a man puts his feet down. His job is to be the intimate lion, the one who can make her feel safe in his arms until they leave the bed.

Clueless to the knife that was stabbing him numb, he blamed himself for not being more than a failure. He hung around to see if he would ever find the way to keep a smile on her face, draining himself of everything good that she would never appreciate.

He became humiliated in the long run after he was introduced to the idea that another man had been fulfilling her wants while he was trying to be what she needed. He then

decided to let the anger stir up a perfect
recipe for bitterness, growing cold as he
dug the grave to bury the good guy he
once was.

The End

If you want him to see the cancer in
the relationship,
help him see his wrongs more than
you are willing to make sure he
hears your complaints.
And before you do so,
please be aware that helping
someone see their wrongs isn't the
same as telling them to get it right.

He has learned that depression is
the mind dwelling on the things
created to hunt him,
until his happiness turns from prey
to a full course meal.
So, he fights.
He has learned to ask the whispers
from demons to find their way out
of his skull,
He puts his insecurity on mute
while clamping a leash on his
anxiety, letting them both know
that it is he who owns his body, not
them.
So, he conquers.

"Overcomer"

People who are in love, yet cheat,
aren't always lying;
some don't know the difference
between love and infatuation.
Almost everyone knows the
beginning stages of love, and
lots of people fall into it.
It is those who reach the different
levels of love who aren't willing to
sacrifice anything to lose that.
Those who only knew infatuation
eventually become infatuated with
someone else.

"Not the love you think."

She is somewhere in the world,
searching for ways to prove to
another man that she deserves the
love he is keeping away from her.

Meanwhile, he is still plotting the
most creative ways to gift his
woman with every bit of the love
those other men could not offer
her.

There are far too many women I
watch put more effort into
searching for the man inside of the
boy, than into finding the woman
they are destined to be.
To those women,
you can only search for a loving
man inside a man;
a boy has to find the man inside
himself.

"Words from the wise."

If you ask him to describe she who has
his heart,
he will say:
That girl is art;
her perfect lips,
her imperfect skin,
the stars on her face called freckles,
the messy hair,
that inviting smile, the boldness that
sits on the throne of her voice.
You can stare at her for eternity and
still not grasp the full beauty of her
existence.

You have dug the words 'I miss you'
out of him so many times, that the
truthfulness of his tongue when he
says it has left long ago.
There are times he misses you, and
there are times he misses the days you
didn't fork out of him the compliments
you wanted to drug your insecurities.
There are times he wishes that he
actually missed you, and that, "I miss
you," wasn't an overused phrase.

He is not his father's misunderstanding
or ego, trying to find women's pride to
leech on.
He is his mother's long-lasting
strength,
her grace,
her softness.
He is the boy who told manhood that it
wants love more than it needs power.

Give me reasons to trust you, and I'll
keep feeding them to my vulnerability
in hopes that it will become full of
enough persuasion to lay a driveway
for love to park itself between us.

Him

You say I am cold on purpose,

but I tell you every part of me that is

looking to be affectionate,

is on pause.

It is on hold until I feel safe,

until I know you will not leave after I

become completely naked and

unprotected with you.

"Precaution"

There are men who if given a second
chance, will be a clinging death that
will eat you away slowly.
But there are men like him who see
second chances as a river of hope to
bring life to the things he first let his
mistakes kill.
Some of us learn our lesson and never
want to take anything for granted
again.

I am still seeking understanding as to
why cheating by a man is blamed on
the fact that he is a man, meanwhile
the same served by a woman is still the
man's fault because he did not keep
happiness on her face and a smile in
her heart.
I thought cheating was ungodly despite
who the sinner was?

They are not more important than you,
they are safer than you.
It is not you versus my guy friends,
it is what is new against what is
established.
My friends have been the greatest form
of loyalty I've known after God, and I
have yet to find myself in a bond
greater than what I have with them.
Help me believe that we'll create as
much laughter with each other as I
have with them.
Let's become best friends naturally
instead of it being an expectation
because we are together.
Let's overcome the hardships time will
lay at our feet.
Besides, I want you to become my best
friend and more.

His nothing

He says he doesn't want a relationship,
wanting to close the book on this love,
but you cannot accept that.
Instead, you beg him to look for a new
chapter. You feed him persuasion until
he second guesses his choices, then
use your body to pull a different tune
out of him. You draw him to be more
indecisive, then frustration grows
deeper in you from his unmade mind,
and anger gains more strength in you
from trying everything and getting
nothing. Then, he closes the book. You
mourn, writing new story lines about
him, letting the world know how he is
the devil with a smile and that your
heart wasn't enough because he is a
blind fool.
When you enter your new chapter in
his life, you write about men like him
being monsters who only know how to

hurt and use. But you leave his story
out. You never ink down that he
wanted a cleaner exit although you
wouldn't grant him that. You carefully
omit the fact that you failed to
persuade him to be stuck in love with
you, casting all blame on him. You
chant that men are no good, and the
evilest manipulative creature there is.
Was there not any self-inflicted pain
there? Did he not warn you that his
heart would not stay?

Boy: No, I can't do this.

Girl: Why? Why are you shooting me down?

Come on.

Boy: Nooooooo!

Girl: Stop being such a punk, you're seriously gonna turn this down?

Through seconds of persistency and minutes of pressuring, Boy breaks and offers his body as a sacrifice to Girl. Besides, it's cool points, cool points he doesn't want, but cool points he can use to fit in.

Girl: No, I can't do this.

Boy: Come on, you know I love you right?

Girl: But I don't want to.

Boy: Come on, if you love me, you'll do it. *continues to touch*

Through seconds of persistency and
minutes of pressuring, Girl breaks and
sacrifices her body to Boy.

Public: Stupid boy, he really tried to
turn down some girl? He must be gay.

Public: Poor girl, that boy is a rapist.
There's no consenting anything to peer
pressure. He is a predator.

"Double Standard"

There is bad and good in everyone and
everything.
You say, "You can't judge a book by
its cover,"
yet you label every book in the same
genre, address them by the same title
because there are similarities in the
plots.
How would you feel if you were
generalized and shoved to fit into a box
you don't belong in?

Pierre Alex Jeanty

Every minute you compare him to
another man,
he learns different reasons why he
should pack up his heart and find his
way to where he meets the standard of
being enough.

It breaks my heart to know the wrongs
men have committed towards women
throughout the timeline of history,
wrongs that should never be justified.

However, it does not give those trying
to rewrite history the right to treat the
men of today as if they are the bad
men of yesterday.

My own father and I can only be
compared as day and night when we
are both observed through the lenses
of fatherhood and husband.
How can we even compare men to men
they have never seen or heard of in
their lives? Yet with a face full of
defensiveness written on it, some of
you scream, "*I am nothing like my
mother!*"

Men may have contributed an ocean of
bad into this world, but this should not
drown the good many men decide to be.

*"Who likes being judged by a past that
isn't even theirs?"*

Until it is understood that men are
creatures with love on their minds and
softness in their hearts,
it will be hard to ever let one of them
love you.
They too travel through mountains to
get to the best version of themselves.
They will always carry a shield until
they see no need for a defense.

You will not always be rewarded love
for being a good man.
Don't be a good man only for the sake
of love, but for the sake of humanity.
Love will eventually give credit where it
is due.

They say, "Without women,
there would be no men," because life
itself would not see daylight on this
earth without them.
Any man who denies that would be a
fool, it is an undeniable truth.
But this truth cannot be weighed on a
balance scale alone.
To leave the other side of it empty, is
to be an unbalanced fool equally.
We must never bury the fact that
without men, life could not be created
inside women.

"Eve needed Adam."

Love him as he is.

When the world seems heavy on his shoulders,
do not first seek ways to help.
Do not search for solutions and constantly
blur out the names of different problems.
It will only awake frustration in him.
Remind him of your existence and
communicate that you are there when needed
without overemphasizing it.
It is not a 'man thing' not want to talk about
it when disappointment is overwhelming and
anger steals the voice.
It happens to all of us.
Therefore, let your existence be his comfort,
your patience be his support,
and your presence his escape from the noise.

"Just be there for him."

Pierre Alex Jeanty

The End

Him

Pierre Alex Jeanty

About the Author

Pierre Alex Jeanty, Founder of
Gentlemenhood™ and CEO of Jeanius
Publishing, is a Haitian-American
author, poet, and influencer who is
devoted to making an impact through
his writing. He primarily focuses on
poetically sharing his journey, lessons,
and mistakes along the paths of
manhood and love. Pierre vows to
share his wisdom with all, in hopes of
inspiring men to become better, and to
be a voice of hope to women who have
lost faith in good men. This is the
vision of his brand, and the agenda he
follows as a writer.

Pierre currently resides in southwest
Florida with his family, and travels as a
speaker as he continues to write. His
library of books written consists of
HER, HER vol. 2, Unspoken Feelings of

Him

*a Gentleman, Unspoken Feelings of a
Gentleman II, To The Women I Once
Loved* and *Apologies That Never Came.*

You can contact him on his website at
pierrealexjeanty.com,
and find him on
Instagram: PierreJeanty
Facebook: Pierre Alex Jeanty
Twitter: PierreAJeanty
and other social media networks by
searching his name.

Pierre Alex Jeanty

<u>Acknowledgments</u>

God, thank you for being the real MVP. I am grateful for this gift and opportunity.

Natalie Jeanty, thank you for believing in me. I love you.

You (the supporter), thank you for valuing my art, my growth, and my journey.